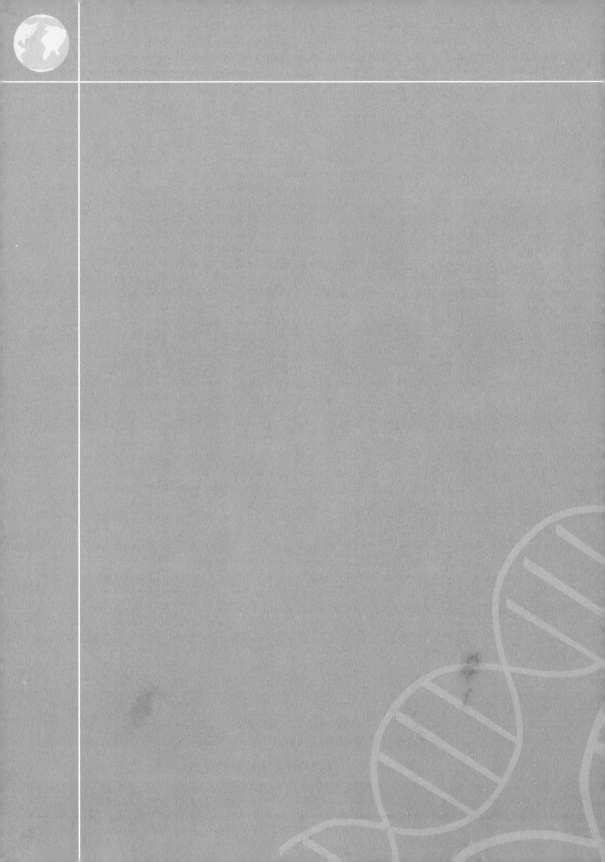

Ecologists:
From Woodward to Miranda

by Debra J. Housel

Science Contributor
Sally Ride Science
Science Consultants
Thomas R. Ciccone, Science Educator
Ronald Edwards, Science Educator

First hardcover edition published in 2009 by
Compass Point Books
151 Good Counsel Drive
P.O. Box 669
Mankato, MN 56002-0669

Editor: Mari Bolte
Designer: Heidi Thompson
Editorial Contributor: Sue Vander Hook

Art Director: LuAnn Ascheman-Adams
Creative Director: Joe Ewest
Editorial Director: Nick Healy
Managing Editor: Catherine Neitge

 This book was manufactured with paper containing at least 10 percent post-consumer waste.

Library of Congress Cataloging-in-Publication Data
Housel, Debra J.
  Ecologists : from Woodward to Miranda / by Debra J. Housel.
     p. cm. — (Mission: Science)
  Includes index.
  ISBN 978-0-7565-4076-0 (library binding)
  1. Ecologists—Biography—Juvenile literature. 2. Ecology—Juvenile literature. I. Title.
  QH26.H68 2008
   577.092'2—dc22
   [B]   2008035733

Visit Compass Point Books on the Internet at *www.compasspointbooks.com*
or e-mail your request to *custserv@compasspointbooks.com*

Table of Contents

Ecologists: Who Are They? 6

John Woodward... 8

Aldo Leopold.. 12

Rachel Carson 15

Ruth Patrick 18

Eugene Odum 20

Jane Lubchenco... 24

Neo Martinez 26

        Ecologists at a Glance 30

        Glossary.. 32

        Ecology Through Time 34

        Additional Resources 38

        Index... 39

        About the Author 40

Ecologists: Who Are They?

What would you do if you saw a crow in your backyard? If you were an ecologist, you would probably find out what it eats—and what might eat it. You would want to know how its food supply limits the number of crows in the area. You would look for animals that compete with the crow for food and nesting materials. And you might also study foxes and hawks, since crows are their prey. Finally you would predict what would happen if all the crows died.

In scientific terms, you are studying the crow's habitat—where it lives. And you are investigating an ecosystem—the way living things in a habitat interact. Ecologists look at the connections living things have with one another and their surroundings. They want to know how things fit together in the natural world.

The word *ecology* was coined in 1866 by German biologist Ernst Haeckel. He defined it as the science of the relationship of an organism to its environment. Today ecologists might study just one part of ecology, such as animal ecology or plant ecology. Sometimes they study the ecology of an entire biome, a large area that shares the same general climate and living organisms.

Early ecologists were known as naturalists—people who studied nature. Much of their work was done through observation. Observing nature remains an important part of ecology today.

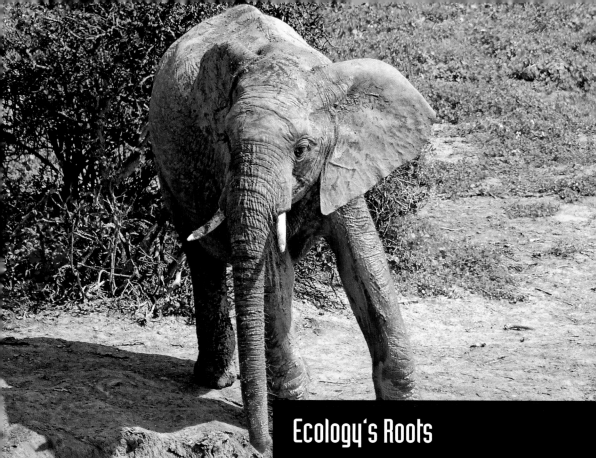

Elephants are the largest land animals. They are also endangered. This has caused some worry among ecologists.

Ecology's Roots

More than 800 years ago, a German nun named Hildegard of Bingen wrote about relationships among humans, plants, animals, and their world. She observed that plants and animals living in an area rely on one another. It was her belief that humans have a duty to take care of Earth. Modern ecologists have come to similar conclusions.

Did You Know?

There are many subdisciplines of ecology, including behavioral, population, community, ecosystem, systems, landscape, evolutionary, and political ecology, as well as ecophysiology.

John Woodward (1665-1728)

John Woodward was a naturalist—he studied plants and animals in their natural surroundings. Today he would be called an ecologist. Because of his curiosity and his experiments, he made some important discoveries. In one experiment, he found that plants grow better in dirty water than in very clean water.

Woodward was born in Derbyshire, England, in 1665. When he was 16, he went to London to study under the physician to King Charles II. While he was a student, he became interested in nature. He studied rocks and minerals, and amassed a large collection of fossils. But his experiment with various types of dirty water was significant. When Woodward was 34 years old, the results of his research were presented to the Royal Society, a highly respected group of scientists.

Woodward had begun his experiment with four glass jars. In each jar he placed a mint plant. He filled one jar with rainwater and another with muddy water from the Thames River, which flows through London. He put drain water into a third jar. He also put drain water in the fourth jar, but he added rotting leaves. He weighed each plant before he began. After a period of 77 days, he weighed them again to determine how much each plant had grown.

Woodward's findings were remarkable:

Jar Contents	Growth
Rainwater	60%
Muddy water	90%
Drain water	125%
Drain water with rotting leaves	310%

Woodward thought the huge growth of the plant in the fourth jar was due to the amount of soil in the water. Now we know that the rotting leaves broke down into nutrients. Then the plant's roots absorbed them, and the plant grew.

Woodward used glass jars and water from various sources in his experiment.

At the Start of the Experiment

muddy water

drain water with rotting leaves

rainwater

drain water

After 77 Days

muddy water

drain water with rotting leaves

rainwater

drain water

It was not normal for the mint plant to more than triple its size in such a short time. If that happened in nature, plants would take over a body of water. Other organisms would compete for the nutrients, but the plants would win. Eventually other living things such as fish would die from lack of sunlight and oxygen. Woodward knew that the result of his experiment was an important discovery.

Too Much Food

When plants receive a lot of extra nutrients, they grow rapidly. When a lawn is fertilized, the grass grows quickly, producing thicker, longer blades. When a

Deadly Algae Blooms

When the population of algae increases rapidly in water (both fresh- and saltwater), it is called algae bloom. Algae colors range from green to yellow to red. Red algae is a type of seaweed found in saltwater. An algae bloom produces a poison that scientists call harmful algae bloom (HAB). Many coastal waters around the world have HABs.

When extra nutrients are dumped in the water, the algae grow rapidly, and more poison is produced. The

algae also use up any extra oxygen in the water, making it harder for marine animals to survive.

Zooplankton are just one of many ocean creatures that are harmed by HABs. These organisms, which range from microscopic in size to large jellyfish or Portuguese man-of-wars, are food for larger fish. When larger fish eat zooplankton that have eaten too much HAB, those fish can also die. When this happens, dead fish will sometimes pile up on shores and beaches.

▲ Pan algae bloom turns the water green in China's Lake Dian.

farmer fertilizes crops, the plants grow taller and healthier.

But sometimes the fertilizer runs off into lakes and ponds. Then water plants such as algae receive too much food. The plants grow at an amazing rate and block sunlight from reaching much below the surface. Plant growth also lowers the water's oxygen levels, eventually suffocating fish until they die. A lake or pond can become an ecological disaster when it has too much food for the plants. Woodward's experiment helped scientists understand plant growth and how it affects its surrounding environment.

Did You Know?

There has been an increase of HABs around the world over the last 30 years. There has also been an increase of new HAB species.

Aldo Leopold (1887-1948)

American ecologist Aldo Leopold grew up with a passion for the outdoors. He was born in Burlington, Iowa, in 1887. He spent summers on Les Cheneaux Islands, a group of 36 small islands along the shores of Lake Huron in upper Michigan. His deep appreciation for nature led him to study at the Yale University School of Forestry. He then worked 19 years for the U.S. Forest Service and spent most of his time in the woods. Later

he worked independently, surveying wildlife in many parts of the United States.

Leopold lived at a time when there were no game laws. If a person wanted to kill an animal, he or she could do it anytime. Leopold was an avid hunter and fisherman, but one hunting experience affected him for the rest of his life. When he was a young man, he shot a wolf. As he watched it die, he felt guilty. The wolf had not threatened him, and he had killed it for no reason. It struck him that every living thing is part of nature, or what we call the ecosystem. He had just damaged the balance of nature without cause.

Leopold began urging others to stop killing animals for no reason. It took him years to convince people that wildlife should be preserved. He fought to get laws passed that would regulate hunting and preserve America's wilderness. He became a leader in the field of wildlife management, pushing for game preserves and national forests. He wanted these areas set aside and protected so they would be there for future generations to enjoy.

Leopold's work helped create two laws more than 20 years after his death in 1948. The National Environmental Policy Act was passed in 1969. It states that the government must think about the environmental effects of any land use before altering or building on a parcel of land. For example, a mall cannot be built without a study to determine whether the project will harm the ecosystem. The second law, the Endangered Species Act of 1973, protects plants, animals, and their ecosystems from becoming extinct.

Leopold died of a heart attack at the age of 61 while helping put out a neighbor's brush fire.

Ranchers used to shoot wolves because they attacked their cattle. The species was near extinction. Laws were passed to make shooting wolves illegal. Without hunting, the wolf population grew back. Now lawmakers are making new laws to allow just enough wolf hunting to keep their numbers balanced.

Lost Birds

Some species of animals have become extinct through the years. When the last animal in a species dies, that type of animal is gone forever from Earth.

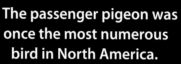

The passenger pigeon was once the most numerous bird in North America. During migration, up to a billion of these birds would fly together in an area about 1 mile (1.6 kilometers) wide and up to 300 miles (500 km) long. By the early 20th century, the passenger pigeon was extinct. For many years these birds had been a favorite target for hunters. Some shot them for sport, and others ate them as a cheap source of food. Eventually they were hunted to extinction. The last passenger pigeon died in 1914 at a zoo in Cincinnati, Ohio. The bird was 29 years old.

Long ago, dodo birds lived on the African island of Mauritius in the Indian Ocean. These flightless birds and their eggs were easy prey for the pigs, dogs, and cats that settlers brought with them to the island. By the last half of the 1600s, there were no more dodo birds on Earth.

Did You Know?

It is estimated that more than 15,500 species of plants and animals are in danger of becoming extinct.

Rachel Carson (1907-1964)

One of the most influential ecologists of the 20th century was Rachel Carson. She was a quiet person who was fascinated with nature's beauty and how it worked. But she—and her book, *Silent Spring*—affected the world in a powerful way through her writings and her passion for preserving and protecting the natural world.

Carson was born in the river town of Springdale, Pennsylvania, on May 27, 1907. She had a simple upbringing and spent time outdoors. She found nature to be fascinating. She also enjoyed books and wanted to become a writer. Her first published writing appeared in a children's magazine when she was just 10 years old.

After high school, Carson attended college and studied marine biology (the study of sea organisms) and zoology (the study of animals).

Notes From *Silent Spring*

"Only within the moment of time represented by the present century has one species—man— acquired significant power to alter the nature of his world."
  –Rachel Carson, *Silent Spring*

"The earth's vegetation is part of a web of life in which there are intimate and essential relations between plants and animals. Sometimes we have no choice but to disturb these relationships, but we should do so thoughtfully, with full awareness that what we do may have consequences remote in time and place."
  –Rachel Carson, *Silent Spring*

She continued to write, working for the Woods Hole Oceanographic Institution and the U.S. Bureau of Fisheries. By the time she was 29, she had risen to editor-in-chief of all publications of the U.S. Fish and Wildlife Service.

Her passion for the natural world came out in pamphlets, articles, and finally books. In 1941, her first book, *Under the Sea-Wind*, was published. Ten years later, she received the National Book Award for *The Sea Around Us*. In 1955, she wrote *The Edge of the Sea*. Her writings interwove the intriguing ocean world teeming with life with the fact that human beings are capable of damaging nature, sometimes permanently. Her books soon made her famous. Some praised her writing, and others criticized her ideas.

The Danger of DDT

DDT was a synthetic pesticide used during World War II. It killed mosquitoes, which carried insect-borne diseases such as malaria and typhus. After the war, it was made available to farmers for their crops.

Carson found that DDT killed more than insects—the birds that ate the insects were also dying. Carson suggested that DDT and other common pesticides caused cancer and were threats not only to wildlife, but to people as well.

Carson became concerned about the use of chemicals that began after World War II ended in 1945. In 1962, she published *Silent Spring*, a book that described the dangers of pesticides such as DDT.

In 1963, Carson testified before the U.S. Congress, urging lawmakers to pass laws that would protect the environment and human health. Carson died of cancer the following year. She was 57. She did not live to see the results of her quiet written campaign to preserve the environment.

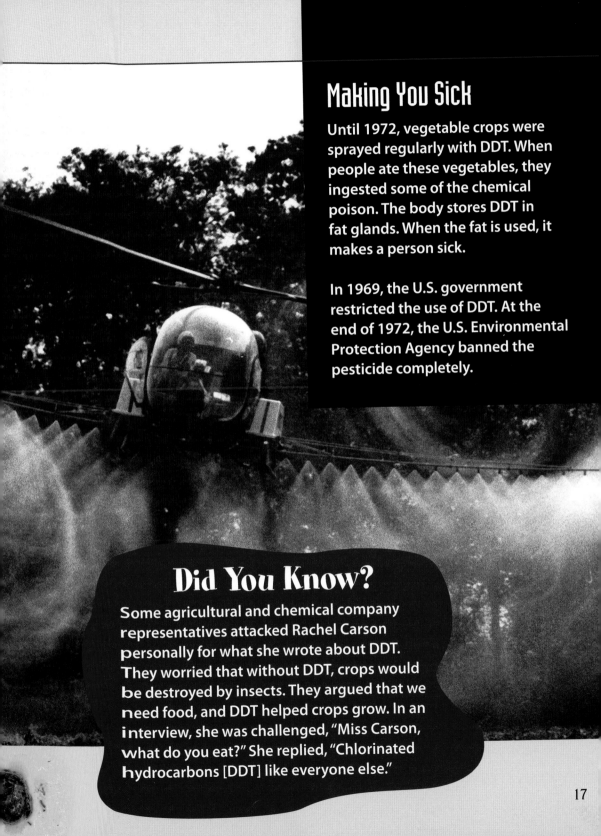

Making You Sick

Until 1972, vegetable crops were sprayed regularly with DDT. When people ate these vegetables, they ingested some of the chemical poison. The body stores DDT in fat glands. When the fat is used, it makes a person sick.

In 1969, the U.S. government restricted the use of DDT. At the end of 1972, the U.S. Environmental Protection Agency banned the pesticide completely.

Did You Know?

Some agricultural and chemical company representatives attacked Rachel Carson personally for what she wrote about DDT. They worried that without DDT, crops would be destroyed by insects. They argued that we need food, and DDT helped crops grow. In an interview, she was challenged, "Miss Carson, what do you eat?" She replied, "Chlorinated hydrocarbons [DDT] like everyone else."

17

Long before protecting the environment was popular, Ruth Patrick was studying water pollution. She worked alongside the government and big industries to make U.S. streams and rivers cleaner and safer. She advised President Lyndon B. Johnson on water pollution and President Ronald Reagan on acid rain.

Patrick was born in Topeka, Kansas, in 1907. She spent much of her childhood outdoors, exploring nature with her father. She later said, "I collected everything: worms and mushrooms and plants and rocks." At the age of 7, she received a microscope. Now she could look at what she collected up close.

Patrick earned her doctorate in botany at the University of Virginia. At the age of 26, she began doing volunteer research for the Academy of Natural Sciences. Her research included the study of diatoms, single-celled algae that are visible only under a microscope. Diatoms are a basic food source for freshwater organisms. The study of inland waters—lakes, ponds, rivers, streams, wetlands, and groundwater—is called limnology.

By studying diatoms, Patrick could determine how clean the water was where the algae lived. Certain types of diatoms prefer certain

Salty Enough?

The Great Salt Lake in northern Utah has a very high concentration of salt. It is far saltier than ocean water. Ruth Patrick proved that the Great Salt Lake was once fresh. She showed that the lake water became salty through evaporation.

18

environments. So she could link their presence or absence to water quality.

To get diatoms, Patrick invented a device called a diatometer. She anchored it to the bottom of the lake or stream she was studying. A cork kept it afloat. As water moved through it, diatoms attached themselves to glass slides in the device. Patrick could then remove the slides and study the diatoms.

Today ecologists still use Patrick's methods. They measure changes in amounts and kinds of plants, animals, and bacteria, which helps

them gauge the impact of pollution.

For 35 years, Patrick taught limnology and botany at the University of Pennsylvania. She has received many awards and served on many environmental boards. She has also written more than 200 scientific papers and several books about the environment.

diatom ➡

⬇ diatometer

Eugene Odum (1913-2002)

Eugene Odum was a pioneer—a pioneer of an idea. He said that studying one species wasn't taking a broad enough view of the world. He saw Earth as a system of interlocking systems that depend on each other to function. He urged people to look at the entire planet as a place where organisms and environments interact to make a healthy Earth.

At first Odum's concept had little support. People doubted that one system depended on another. But today what is called ecosystem ecology is an accepted science throughout the world. Odum is sometimes called the father of modern ecology.

Odum was born on September 17, 1913, in Newport, New Hampshire. But he spent his childhood in Chapel Hill, North Carolina. His father, sociologist Howard W. Odum, taught him to look at the world as a whole—to take a holistic approach.

Odum attended college and received a doctorate in zoology from the University of Illinois. In 1940, he returned to the South where he became a biology professor at the University of Georgia. He kept that position for 40 years.

Although Odum taught about ecology in his biology class, he saw an urgent need to make ecology a course of its own. But there was no ecology textbook. In 1953, Odum wrote *Fundamentals of Ecology*, a textbook that is still considered "the book" for the study of ecology. The book states that we should look at climate, plants, and animals to learn how the pieces fit together. His book showed people how to study the ways living things are interrelated.

In the early 1950s, Odum was also working on a team with ecologist Ruth Patrick. The team gathered data about the water quality and

It is easy to find various organisms—plants and animals—interacting.

21

organisms in the Savannah River, which forms the border between Georgia and South Carolina. Odum showed that the individual parts of our environment (animals, plants, water, air) not only work together, but also affect each other.

Odum was the first scientist to study salt marsh plants and animals. He learned about organisms that adapt to the salty water that the ocean tides push onto coastal grassy areas. He found out that they all use the same nutrients and the same elements, such as carbon and nitrogen. His research on salt marshes led to laws that protect these areas called wetlands.

Odum died on August 10, 2002, at the age of 89. But even after his death, his work continued. Countless scientists who learned from him have taken his ideas and research even further. Many consider Odum the most important ecologist of the 20th century.

▼ Salt Marsh Nature Center in New York

Important Wetlands

Wetlands are areas where the soil is soaked with moisture. Swamps, marshes, and bogs are wetlands. They are ideal places for unique types of plants that can only survive in soggy, wet soil.

Swamps are areas of low-lying water that experience flooding from time to time. The water may be freshwater or saltwater. The huge variety of swamp vegetation includes trees, thick shrubs, and woody underbrush. Diverse animals live there, including frogs and alligators.

Marsh water is shallower than swamp water. Vegetation is grassy, and the water can be fresh or salty. The water either moves slowly or not at all. Marshes are home to a wide variety of plant and animal life. Rice grows well in the low-lying waters of marshes. Salt marshes are near oceans and rely on the tides to cover the area with water. When water rushes out of the marsh, it takes dead plants and animals with it. This carries necessary nutrients into the sea.

Bogs are areas of wet, spongy ground full of dead plants, usually peat moss. Bogs offer a special environment for certain plants and animals. Berries such as blueberries and cranberries grow well in bogs.

Nearly a third of America's endangered species live in wetlands. Many wetlands are at risk or have already been destroyed. People sometimes fill in wetlands to build houses, cities, parking lots, or farms. Other times they flood them to create recreational lakes. When these things happen, many animals lose the only ecosystem in which they can survive. In the United States, some wetlands are protected by the federal government.

Jane Lubchenco (1947-   )

Many scientists think that greenhouse gases have raised Earth's atmospheric and oceanic temperatures. This global warming will cause many species to become extinct. Jane Lubchenco brought this problem to the public's attention and explained it in a way that people could understand it.

Lubchenco was born in 1947 and raised in Denver, Colorado. She received a doctorate in marine ecology from Harvard University and then taught there for two years. In 1978, she became a zoology professor at Oregon State University.

Lubchenco studies the ecosystem of the ocean on the West Coast of the United States. She works with a team that studies how the ocean is changing. She also finds out how changes in climate and

A dead zone doesn't allow life to prosper.

other ecosystems affect the ocean and ocean life.

Part of Lubchenco's work is to let the world know what is happening to our ecosystems. She often addresses the U.S. Congress, the United Nations, and other groups to recommend ways to reduce the world's greenhouse gases.

She is also concerned about the world's coral reefs. She fears that they all will die within the next 50 years. Her work has also taken her to lakes where she has discovered what are called "dead zones"—places where no fish live. She has found 40 dead zones, caused by algae blooms that rob the water of sunlight and oxygen. Each zone is near the mouth of a river that has fertilizer runoff.

Lubchenco's efforts have made the environment an important political issue. She stresses that we must take better care of our Earth.

It's Alive!

Coral reefs are alive. They are made of living organisms found in shallow sea waters. When these organisms grow on top of each other, they form a colorful ridge of rocks and coral called a reef. Some of the largest reefs in the world have taken half a million years to form.

Jane Lubchenco once taught a class on coral reefs in Jamaica. When she returned more than 10 years later, she found the reefs ruined. Some people had dropped bombs into the reef to catch more fish.

Pollution is a problem for coral reefs. Water pollution blocks the sunlight needed for algae, the food for living reef organisms. When the algae die, the organisms starve. A dead coral reef turns white and never recovers.

Neo Martinez (1958-)

Neo Martinez is an expert on food webs—the complex system of what eats what in an ecosystem. Martinez created a way to picture food webs and explain them. Through his continuing research, he identifies the basic things that all ecosystems share. He studies the ways living organisms are tied to each other and their ecosystems.

Martinez's father was the first Mexican-American in the United States to receive a doctorate in the physical sciences. He passed along his love of science to his son. Neo Martinez received his doctorate in energy and resources in 1991 from the University of California at Berkeley, where he later became a professor.

One of the unique things about Martinez's research is that he recorded it on a computer. Eventually Martinez created a computer model for food webs. In 1999, he received a grant from the National Science Foundation to develop the Instructional Environmental Science Computer Lab at Berkeley.

Martinez enjoys making science practical for his students. He said, "I really want to encourage students to develop themselves, and to learn to be perceptive and critical thinkers about the world around them." His students have used the lab to make their own computer models of food webs.

One of the main things Martinez discovered is that many more animals than we thought are omnivores. Omnivores eat both plants and animals. People once thought that most animals were either meat eaters or plant eaters.

Martinez also found that small food webs are very fragile. The removal or addition of a species can make the whole ecosystem unbalanced. For example, the Arctic food web is small. Algae that grow on the bottom of the ice provide food for zooplankton. In turn, the zooplankton are food for small fish, which are eaten by arctic cod. Ringed seals eat the cod, and polar

Arctic Food Web

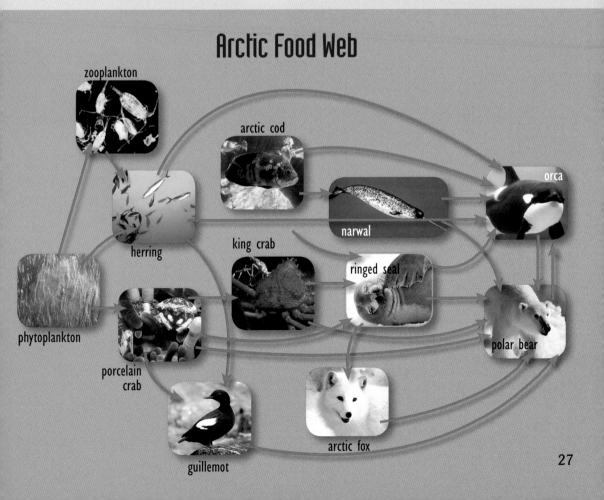

zooplankton

arctic cod

orca

narwal

herring

king crab

ringed seal

phytoplankton

porcelain crab

polar bear

guillemot

arctic fox

Predator or Prey?

Most animals eat more than one kind of food. Then those animals are often eaten by more than one kind of predator. Visualize a drawing of all the plants and animals in an area such as a forest. Now mentally draw lines from each one to all the organisms it eats. You will end up with a very complicated web of lines, called a food web.

Most animals are predators of some animals; they are prey for others. For example, a wolf is the predator of deer, moose, and elk. Since it is at the top of the food chain, it has few predators. But it is prey for parasites such as heartworms. A parasite is an animal that lives off of another animal's body. The parasite can sometimes kill its host.

⬆ A tick is a common parasite.

bears eat the seals. This food web is in danger because the Arctic is warming up. As ice melts, fewer algae grow, a small event that could put the entire ecosystem at risk.

People have caused entire food webs to change by bringing just one new species into an ecosystem. An alien species, as it is called, spreads quickly. For example, brown tree snakes once were unknowingly taken onto a ship at their home on the coast of Australia. They traveled to the island of Guam. After they arrived, no animals wanted to eat them, and their numbers grew out of control. They wiped out many native birds, small mammals, and lizards.

Lake Victoria in Africa now has a plant originally from Brazil. The water hyacinth grows out of control. The small floating plants with beautiful purple flowers grew so rapidly that they filled up this second largest lake in the world. The plants looked like a huge blanket over the water. Fish died, boats got trapped, and people couldn't fish. People began looking for ways to get rid of the plants. Some scientists put insects in the water. They fed exclusively on water hyacinth, but they didn't kill the plants. People also used huge machines to chop up the plants. Scientists continue to search for ways to get rid of this alien invader.

Energy Pyramid

An energy pyramid shows the exchange of energy among organisms in an ecosystem. The bottom of the pyramid is made of producers, which are usually plants. The plants provide food and energy for primary consumers such as zebras and gazelles. The primary consumers, in turn, provide food and energy for secondary consumers such as lions.

It takes a lot of food to feed the apex predators, the animals at the top of the pyramid. For example, in one year, it takes nearly 7,500 tons (6,800 metric tons) of grass in an area to keep 60 tons (54 metric tons) of primary consumers such as deer or sheep alive. And all those primary consumers keep just one 450-pound (204-kg) lion alive.

Energy decreases as you move up the pyramid. Every time something gets eaten, energy is lost (usually it is turned into heat). There is only enough energy for a few animals at the top.

When looking at an energy pyramid, keep in mind that it doesn't tell the whole story as a food web does. Many more plants and animals are involved in the exchange of energy in an ecosystem than the plants and animals that are shown in an energy pyramid.

Rachel Carson

Fields of study: *Marine biology, the environment*

Known for: *Author of* Silent Spring, *which drew public attention to environmental problems; worked to reduce use of DDT*

Nationality: *American*

Birthplace: *Springdale, Pennsylvania*

Date of birth: *May 27, 1907*

Date of death: *April 14, 1964*

Awards and honors: *National Book Award, 1951; Presidential Medal of Freedom, 1980; Rachel Carson Bridge in Pittsburgh, Pennsylvania, is named in her honor*

Aldo Leopold

Fields of study: *Ecology, forestry*

Known for: *Author of* A Sand County Almanac; *helped develop environmental ethics*

Nationality: *American*

Birthplace: *Burlington, Iowa*

Date of birth: *January 11, 1887*

Date of death: *April 21, 1948*

Awards and honors: *Founder of the Wilderness Society in 1935; the Aldo Leopold Wilderness in New Mexico is named for him*

Jane Lubchenco

Fields of study: *Environmental science, marine ecology*

Nationality: *American*

Birthplace: *Denver, Colorado*

Date of birth: *December 4, 1947*

Awards and honors: *2002 Heinz Award in the Environment; Nierenberg Prize for Science in the Public Interest in 2003*

(from Scripps Institution of Oceanography); 2004 Environmental Law Institute Award; 2005 American Association for the Advancement of Science's Award for Public Understanding of Science and Technology

Neo Martinez

Field of study: *Food webs*

Known for: *Director of the Pacific Ecoinformatics and Computational Ecology Lab (PEACE Lab)*

Nationality: *Mexican-American*

Date of birth: *1958*

Awards and honors: *Several National Science Foundation grants to create instructional labs; sponsored the first chapter of the Society for the Advancement of Chicano and Native American Scientists*

Eugene Odum

Field of study: *Ecosystem ecology*

Known for: *Furthering the concept of the ecosystem*

Nationality: *American*

Birthplace: *Newport, New Hampshire*

Date of birth: *September 17, 1913*

Date of death: *August 10, 2002*

Awards and honors: *Crafoord Prize from the Royal Swedish Academy of Sciences, 1987; elected member of the National Academy of Sciences, 1970; French prize from the Institute de la Vie, 1975; Tyler Ecology Award (presented by President Jimmy Carter, 1977)*

Ruth Patrick

Fields of study: *Botany, limnology*

Known for: *Research of diatoms and freshwater ecology*

Nationality: *American*

Birthplace: *Topeka, Kansas*

Date of birth: *November 26, 1907*

Awards and honors: *National Medal of Science, 1996; elected to the American Philosophical Society in 1974; recipient of 25 honorary degrees and the Philadelphia Award in 1973, and National Medal of Science from President Clinton in 1996*

John Woodward

Fields of study: *Nature, geology*

Known for: *Water experiments with mint plants*

Nationality: *English*

Birthplace: *Derbyshire, England*

Date of birth: *May 1, 1665*

Date of death: *April 25, 1728*

Awards and honors: *Fellow of the Royal Society, 1693*

algae bloom—heavy growth of algae in or on a body of water; it cuts down on the sunlight and oxygen available to aquatic life; caused by too many nutrients in the water

biome—large area that shares the same general climate and living organisms

carbon dioxide (CO_2)—gas in the air that animals give off and plants use to make food; greenhouse gas in the air that traps heat from the sun

climate—typical weather conditions in a particular area

coral reef—ecosystem found in warm, shallow parts of the ocean; chain of rocks and coral that provides a home for thousands of sea animals

DDT—pesticide used to kill harmful insects, also causing the deaths of animals further up the food chain; banned in the United States

dead zone—area in a pond, lake, or ocean where no marine life can live

deforestation—loss of trees in forested areas because of industrial or agricultural use

diatoms—single-celled algae that live in fresh water

diatometer—device for collecting diatoms

ecologist—scientist who studies ecology

ecology—science that looks at the connections that living things have with one another and their surroundings

ecosystem—interactions in a community of plants and animals living in a natural environment

endangered—threatened with extinction

extinction—permanent absence of a species

fertilizer—substance put on fields or lawns to make crops or grass grow better, usually containing nutrients

food web—series of connecting links that show what eats what in an ecosystem

fossil fuels—fuels, including coal, oil, and natural gas, made from the remains of ancient organisms

game—wild animals, birds, and fish hunted for food or sport

game laws—restrictions on the hunting, trapping, or capture of wild game

global warming—rising temperature of Earth caused by increasing amounts of carbon dioxide and other greenhouse gases in the atmosphere

greenhouse effect—warming effect that happens when certain gases in Earth's atmosphere absorb heat and thereby make the air warmer

greenhouse gases—gases present in the atmosphere that reduce the loss of Earth's heat into space and contribute to global warming

Harmful Algae Bloom (HAB)—saltwater algae that poison the animals that consume them

habitat—natural home of an animal or plant

heartworm—parasite that lives in the heart of its host and eventually kills it

host—plant or animal from which a parasite gets its nutrition

limnology—study of freshwater ecosystems

national park—reserve of land owned and protected by a national government

naturalist—person who studies plants and animals in their natural surroundings

omnivore—animal that eats both plants and animals

ozone—form of oxygen that exists in Earth's atmosphere in small amounts; contributes in a small way to the greenhouse effect

parasite—plant or animal that gets its food by living on or inside another plant or animal

pesticide—substance or mixture of substances used to kill harmful organisms

predator—animal that hunts and eats other animals (for example, a toad is an insect's predator)

prey—animal that is eaten by another

salt marsh—low-lying grassy wetland that is frequently flooded with salt water

wetlands—large area of land covered with swamps, marshes, or bogs

zooplankton—tiny animal organism that drifts in great numbers in fresh- or saltwater

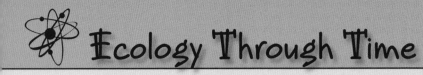

6,000 B.C.	Villages in southern Israel and Jordan collapse because of deforestation
400 B.C.	Greek physician Hippocrates writes *On Airs, Waters, and Places*, the earliest known work on human ecology
100 A.D.	Chinese invent insecticide using a powder of dried chrysanthemum flowers
1774	John Chapman, also known as Johnny Appleseed, is born; for years, he planted apple trees across the Midwest
1785	John James Audubon, wildlife artist and author of *Birds of America*, is born
1804	Nicholas de Saussure discovers that plants need carbon dioxide from the air and nitrogen from the soil
1853	Planning begins for Central Park, the first landscaped public park in the United States
1859	Charles Darwin publishes the first edition of *The Origin of Species*, in which he proposes a theory of evolution in nature
1872	Yellowstone National Park, the first national park in America, is established
1890	Yosemite, Kings Canyon (formerly known as General Grant), and Sequoia National Parks are established
1891	Congress passes the Forest Reserve Act, with the objective of keeping some land under federal ownership. By the end of 1893, 17.5 million acres (7 million hectares) are set aside in forest reserves

1895	The National Trust is founded in Great Britain to preserve historic buildings and monuments and places of historical interest or natural beauty
1896	Svante Arrhenius first suggests that the use of fossil fuel is the cause of global warming; his theory is later known as the greenhouse effect
1898	The Rivers and Harbors Act bans pollution of navigable waters in the United States
1901	John Muir publishes *Our National Parks*, a collection of essays urging conservation
1902	The population of American bison drops to fewer than 800 animals (from a population of more than 40 million a century before); 21 bison are placed under government protection in Yellowstone National Park
1903	President Theodore Roosevelt organizes the first National Bird Preserve; by 1909, he has created 42 million acres (17 million hectares) of national forests and more than 50 national wildlife refuges
1905	Audubon Society is founded, with the goal of conserving and restoring natural ecosystems
1908	Chlorination is first used to treat water, making the water 10 times purer than when filtered
1916	The U.S. National Park Service is established
1934	Russian ecologist G.F. Gause determines that two similar species cannot occupy the same ecosystem for long periods of time; called Gause's principle

1935	U.S. Soil Conservation Service is established
1937	Glen Thomas Trewartha coins the term *greenhouse effect*
1938	The National Wildlife Federation is formed
1956	The Water Pollution Control Act makes federal money available for water treatment plants
1962	Rachel Carson publishes *Silent Spring*, a look at the dangers of the unchecked use of pesticides
1970	The Clean Air Act is amended, toughening regulations but not controlling acid rain and airborne toxic chemicals
1972	DDT, a pesticide that caused a decline in several bird species, is phased out in the United States
1976	Studies show that chlorofluorocarbons in spray cans contribute to the decrease in the ozone
1978	Residents are evacuated from Love Canal, New York, after a major chemical waste dump is discovered
1979	The Three Mile Island nuclear power plant in Pennsylvania experiences a near meltdown
1986	The Chernobyl nuclear power plant in the Soviet Union experiences a massive failure, contaminating large areas of the surrounding region and northern Europe
1987	The Montreal Protocol is signed, reducing the use of chlorofluorocarbons and phasing them out by the end of the century

1988	Radon contamination is found to be more prevalent in U.S. homes than previously thought
1989	The *Exxon Valdez* oil tanker crashes off the coast of Alaska, spilling as much as 11 million gallons (42 million liters) of crude oil; two decades later, scientists are still finding spilled oil
1990	Scientists determine that 1990 is the warmest year on record
1991	The United States agrees to protect Antarctica from mineral excavation and to preserve the region's native flora and fauna
1992	Small amounts of ozone depletion are reported for the first time in the Northern Hemisphere
1993	The ozone hole over Antarctica reaches record size; its growth is thought to be the continuing result of the volcanic eruption of Mount Pinatubo in the Philippines
2001	President Bill Clinton protects more land for wildlife conservation than did Presidents Theodore Roosevelt and Jimmy Carter
2005	The Kyoto Protocol takes effect; most countries agree to restrict their greenhouse gas emissions by set amounts; the United States refuses to sign the agreement
2006	Former U.S. Vice President Al Gore releases *An Inconvenient Truth*, a documentary film discussing global warming
2008	The state of Florida purchases 187,000 acres (74,800 hectares) of land from the United States' largest sugar refinery in an attempt to save the Everglades

Carson, Rachel. *Silent Spring*. Boston: Houghton Mifflin, 1994.

Jackson, Tom. *Tropical Forests*. Austin, Texas: Raintree Publishers, 2003.

Nardo, Don. *Climate Crisis: The Science of Global Warming*. Minneapolis: Compass Point Books, 2008.

Steele, Christy. *Grassland Animals*. Austin, Texas: Raintree Steck-Vaughn Publishers, 2002.

Stille, Darlene. *The Greenhouse Effect: Warming the Planet*. Minneapolis: Compass Point Books, 2006.

Stille, Darlene. *Nature Interrupted: The Science of Environmental Chain Reactions*. Minneapolis: Compass Point Books, 2008

On the Web

For more information on this topic, use FactHound.

1. Go to *www.facthound.com*
2. Choose your grade level.
3. Begin your search.

This book's ID number is 9780756540760

FactHound will find the best sites for you.

Index

algae bloom, 10, 11, 25

biome, 6

Carson, Rachel, 15–16, 17
climate, 24
coral reefs, 25

DDT, 16, 17
dead zones, 25
diatom, 18–19
diatometer, 19

ecologist, 6, 8, 12, 15, 19,
    21, 22
ecology, 6, 7, 20–21, 24
ecosystem, 6, 12, 13, 20, 24,
    25, 26, 27, 28, 29
Endangered Species
    Act, 13
energy pyramid, 29
environment, 6, 20, 22
extinct, 14

fertilizer, 10–11, 25
food web, 26, 27, 28

game, 12–13
game laws, 12,
global warming, 24
greenhouse gas, 24, 25

habitat, 6

Leopold, Aldo, 12–13
limnology, 18, 19
Lubchenco, Jane, 24–25

Martinez, Neo, 26–27

National Environmental
    Policy Act, 13
naturalist, 8
nutrient, 9, 10

Odum, Eugene, 20–22
omnivores, 27
organism, 6, 10, 15, 20, 22,
    25, 26, 28, 29

parasite, 28
Patrick, Ruth, 18–19, 21
predator, 28, 29
prey, 14, 28

Silent Spring, 15, 16

U.S. Forestry Service, 12

wetlands, 22, 23
wildlife, 12, 13, 16
Woodward, John, 8–9

zoology, 15, 20, 24

Debra J. Housel

Debra Housel earned a master's degree from Nazareth College in Rochester, New York, and worked as a teacher for more than a dozen years before becoming a freelance writer. She has written more than 80 titles for the education market, some of them award-winning. Debra is an avid environmentalist, and she appreciates the beauties of the natural world. She lives in Rochester, New York, where she enjoys being outdoors and observing the world around her.

Image Credits